The Big Questions for Mom

for Mom

Finding Common Ground,
Bonding and Creating a Family
Heirloom Together

A Guided Journal

Robert K. Elder & Sasha Schwenk

The Big Questions

By Robert K. Elder and Sasha Schwenk

©2023 Odd Hours Media

Published by Odd Hours Media

Cover Design: Muhammad Hassan Khalid and Madeline Nathaus

Typesetting: Madeline Nathaus

Illustrations: Eva Elder

A CIP record for this book is available from the Library of Congress Cataloging-in-Publication Data

ISBN: 978-1-955641-03-6

Printed in the USA

For our parents.

INTRODUCTION

This book started with a conversation.

Two of them, actually.

I've been interviewing loved ones for years, recording family stories and history, but with very little organization. I've published story-prompt books, but never got quite what I had in mind: an easy way to connect, laugh and collect personal stories. After all, when we know our parents' history, we can understand the culture and influences that shaped them and, by extension, ourselves.

Sasha Schwenk, my longtime friend and co-author, was feeling the same way.

"My father and I were catching up recently, and he casually tossed out a story I'd never heard before from his childhood," she said. "My jaw dropped, and I demanded to know more. The story unfolded, leading to more unheard-of snippets and revelations. I had taken Dad's stories for granted, thinking I'd known all there was to know about him, and here he was with a rich and revealing chapter."

This led to the second conversation, between Sasha and me. Why isn't it easier to truly connect with those we love the most? When we first started talking about this book series, we were looking for a way to bridge the gap between generations. Moreover, in the digital age, family histories are often lost. Add to that deepening political divisions, living far apart and a pandemic—all of these factors contributed to a sense of urgency.

With *The Big Questions* journal series, we wanted to encourage conversations, build empathy and compassion, and foster honest dialog between generations. This book starts out chronologically, with straightforward questions about childhood and family. It eases into more challenging and thought-provoking territory, designed to prompt storytelling, not just information sharing.

The Big Questions helps family members to actively listen to one another, to remind them of the values they have in common. Our strategy is to create a homemade memoir series and lasting record of family stories in which our loved ones tell the stories that matter the most. The results have surprised us, and we hope they'll surprise you.

Have fun. Listen. And ask more questions.

— Robert K. Elder, 2023

CONTENTS

CHILDHOOD

What is your first memory?

CHILDHOOD

Describe your childhood bedroom.

CHILDHOOD

Describe the house you grew up in.

CHILDHOOD

What was your secret hiding place in your house, and what did you hide in it?

CHILDHOOD

Describe your neighborhood.

CHILDHOOD

How did you get to school?
What did you encounter along your route?

CHILDHOOD

What were your favorite Halloween costumes as a kid?

Did you have a favorite or celebratory family meal? Or a restaurant where you were regulars?

CHILDHOOD

Describe a place you traveled to on
vacation with your family as a child.

CHILDHOOD

Did you have any hobbies?
What drew you to them?

Did you have any collections? How did your collection get started? What did it mean to you? Do you still have any part of that collection?

CHILDHOOD

Did you play any organized sports?
Describe a thrilling victory or a
humiliating defeat.

CHILDHOOD

What did you learn from playing on a team?

CHILDHOOD

As a kid, what did you want to be when you grew up?

Did you have a favorite school
subject or teacher? Please elaborate.

CHILDHOOD

Describe your childhood best friend.

CHILDHOOD

Did you have an imaginary friend?
What did they look like, and
what did you do together?

CHILDHOOD

Describe your first crush.

....
....
....
....
....
....
....
....
....
....
....
....
....
....
....
....
....
....

Describe your relationships with your siblings or relatives close to your age.

CHILDHOOD

Did you ever pull any pranks or practical
jokes? If yes, please describe them.

....

....

....

....

....

....

....

....

....

....

....

....

....

....

....

....

....

CHILDHOOD

Were you ever the victim of any pranks?
What happened?

CHILDHOOD

Did you ever get into a fight as a child?
What happened?

CHILDHOOD

Did you have a childhood bully?
Was the relationship ever resolved?

CHILDHOOD

Who was the bad seed in your
neighborhood? Was it you?
Please elaborate.

CHILDHOOD

Were you ever admitted to the hospital as a child? What happened?

CHILDHOOD

Tell a story about a time you got in trouble
as a kid (that you can laugh at now).

Did you ever consider running away from home? Why, and what happened?

CHILDHOOD

What was your childhood bogeyman?
What were you afraid of?

....

....

....

....

....

....

....

....

....

....

....

....

....

....

....

....

....

....

....

CHILDHOOD

How did you overcome
your childhood fears?

What traditions did your family have
for events like birthdays or holidays?

CHILDHOOD

What family story do you remember differently from everyone else?

CHILDHOOD

Describe your mother.

....

....

....

....

....

....

....

....

....

....

....

....

....

....

....

....

....

....

CHILDHOOD

What was your relationship with her like?

CHILDHOOD

Describe your father.

....
....
....
....
....
....
....
....
....
....
....
....
....
....
....
....
....
....
....

CHILDHOOD

What was your relationship with him like?

How did your parents show that they loved you?

How did your parents praise you?

CHILDHOOD

What did your parents teach you about
marriage and commitment?
What did you observe?

....

....

....

....

....

....

....

....

....

....

....

....

....

....

....

....

....

CHILDHOOD

Did your parents separate or divorce when
you were young? What immediate
changes occurred in your life as a result?

....

....

....

....

....

....

....

....

....

....

....

....

....

....

....

....

....

....

....

CHILDHOOD

What did your parents tell you about sex?

CHILDHOOD

Did your parents ever lie to you to protect you?

CHILDHOOD

What did your parents tell you about death?

TEEN YEARS

Describe yourself as a teenager.

What did you think was cool?
What made you feel cool?

TEEN YEARS

What fashion choice do you now regret?

How did you earn spending money?
What did you spend it on?

....

....

....

....

....

....

....

....

....

....

....

....

....

....

....

....

....

....

....

What were your grades like?
What subjects were you best in?

TEEN YEARS

Was there a movie or book that changed your view of the world? How?

Who was your favorite actor or actress? Why?

TEEN YEARS

Tell a story about your first date.

....

....

....

....

....

....

....

....

....

....

....

....

....

....

....

....

....

....

TEEN YEARS

Who was your first kiss? How did it go?

TEEN YEARS

What fun thing would you never do again?

TEEN YEARS

What was your worst moment in
high school? How did you cope?

TEEN YEARS

What do you wish you would've done when you were younger?

....

....

....

....

....

....

....

....

....

....

....

....

....

....

....

....

....

....

Did you have a curfew?
If so, did you ever break it?
What happened, and was it worth it?

Did you know anyone in childhood or in
your teens who died, who was your age?

If yes, how did you or your community deal with it?

How did you differ politically
from your parents?

What beliefs did your parents hold when
you were growing up that you did not?

TEEN YEARS

What did you knowingly do to annoy your parents?

....

....

....

....

....

....

....

....

....

....

....

....

....

....

....

....

....

....

If you had a recurring conflict with your parents, what was it about?

RELATIONSHIPS

Who was the first person to break your heart? What happened?

....

....

....

....

....

....

....

....

....

....

....

....

....

....

....

....

....

....

....

RELATIONSHIPS

What event signaled the end of a relationship for you?

RELATIONSHIPS

Do you believe in love at first sight?
Have you ever experienced it?
What are the pros and cons?

RELATIONSHIPS

Who did you know was bad for you, but
you dated or hung out with anyway?

RELATIONSHIPS

What advice did your parents give you about relationships? Was it good advice?

RELATIONSHIPS

What advice did your parents give you about arguing or fighting?

RELATIONSHIPS

Did you have relatives other than your parents who were good role models or bad influences?

....
....
....
....
....
....
....
....
....
....
....
....
....
....
....
....
....

RELATIONSHIPS

Outside of your immediate family, which family members were you closest to?

RELATIONSHIPS

Tell me a story about a
memorable roommate.

··
··
··
··
··
··
··
··
··
··
··
··
··
··
··
··
··
··

Did you have a mentor figure?
How did they help you

CAREER

What was your first job?
What did you learn from it?

CAREER

Were you ever fired from a job?
Or quit dramatically?

CAREER

What was the job that you wanted that you got?

. . . .

. . . .

. . . .

. . . .

. . . .

. . . .

. . . .

. . . .

. . . .

. . . .

. . . .

. . . .

. . . .

. . . .

. . . .

HELLO
my name is:

. . . .

. . . .

. . . .

CAREER

What was the job you wanted but ended up not getting?

CAREER

What did you imagine that your career would be? How did it get from Point A to Point B?

....
....
....
....
....
....
....
....
....
....
....
....
....
....
....
....
....

CAREER

What achievement are you most proud of, career-wise?

CAREER

Is there a career you wish you tried?
What was it, and why didn't you pursue it?

....

....

....

....

....

....

....

....

....

....

....

....

....

....

....

....

....

....

CAREER

What do all of your jobs have in common?

HUMOR

What will you always find funny?

Tell a joke that made you laugh out loud.

HUMOR

What were the times in your life
when you have laughed the hardest?
What was the trigger?

....

....

....

....

....

....

....

....

....

....

....

....

....

....

....

....

....

Did your family have their own
special vocabulary or sayings?

HUMOR

Explain some of your inside jokes.

HUMOR

What informed your sense of humor?

HA!

PHILOSOPHY

What ideals form your personal philosophy?

....

....

....

....

....

....

....

....

....

....

....

....

....

....

....

....

....

....

PHILOSOPHY

Where do you stand on free-will versus predestination?

PHILOSOPHY

If you had a personal crest,
what symbols would be on it?

PHILOSOPHY

If you had a personal motto,
what would it be?

PHILOSOPHY

Are you more likely to give advice or take advice? Why?

....

....

....

....

....

....

....

....

....

....

....

....

....

....

....

....

....

....

PHILOSOPHY

Is there a philosophical problem that
rattles around in your head?

STORIES

Tell a story about a time you
had a prayer answered.

....

....

....

....

....

....

....

....

....

....

....

....

....

....

....

....

....

....

Tell a story about a time you're glad
that a prayer went unanswered.

STORIES

Tell a story about your worst hangover.

Have you ever almost died? Tell the story.

STORIES

What opportunity did you not take advantage of?

Have you ever been arrested?
Or have a tense interaction with law
enforcement?

STORIES

Describe a life-changing interaction you had with a stranger.

....

....

....

....

....

....

....

....

....

....

....

....

....

....

....

....

....

....

STORIES

Tell a story about an epiphany moment.

STORIES

What's the most important letter you have ever received?

How has technology changed your life?
Please elaborate.

....
....
....
....
....
....
....
....
....
....
....
....
....
....
....
....
....
....

Describe a time you made a difference in someone's life.

....

....

....

....

....

....

....

....

....

....

....

....

....

....

....

....

....

....

STORIES

What is your favorite photo of yourself? Why?

Has your life turned out differently
from what you expected? How so?

....

....

....

....

....

....

....

....

....

....

....

....

....

....

....

....

....

....

If you told your younger self about your
life, what would be hard to believe?

STORIES

Are you superstitious about anything?

....

....

....

....

....

....

....

....

....

....

....

....

....

....

....

....

....

....

What prompted the superstition? Did you inherit it from your family?

What is a song or lyric that best describes you or your life?

STORIES

Do you have a treasured family heirloom?
What is it, and why is it special to you?

Have you ever had a lucid dream, one
in which you could control what was
happening? Describe the experience.

....

....

....

....

....

....

....

....

....

....

....

....

....

....

....

....

....

....

Describe a recurring nightmare.
When did you have it? How did it stop,
or does it occasionally still pop up?

What or who formed your life in ways you could not have predicted?

....

....

....

....

....

....

....

....

....

....

....

....

....

....

....

....

....

....

STORIES

What experiences changed you most from childhood to adulthood?

Describe your first voting
experience. What were the issues that
mattered to you most?

· ·

· ·

· ·

· ·

· ·

· ·

· ·

· ·

· ·

· ·

· ·

· ·

· ·

· ·

· ·

· ·

STORIES

Did you ever vote for someone
and regret it later?

115

Have you ever stuck up for anybody in a
public confrontation? What happened?

....

....

....

....

....

....

....

....

....

....

....

....

....

....

....

....

....

....

HINDSIGHT

What advice would you give to your younger self?

....

....

....

....

....

....

....

....

....

....

....

....

....

....

....

....

....

....

HINDSIGHT

Who gave you advice that's been most valuable? What was the advice?

HINDSIGHT

If you could relive one day, what day would that be?

HINDSIGHT

What memory can still make you cringe?

HINDSIGHT

If you could go back in time and change
one thing, what would it be?

HINDSIGHT

Tell a story about a lie you still regret.

· ·

· ·

· ·

· ·

· ·

· ·

· ·

· ·

· ·

· ·

· ·

· ·

· ·

· ·

· ·

· ·

· ·

HINDSIGHT

Tell a story about a lie you got away with. Was it worth it?

HINDSIGHT

Tell a story about a time you told
the truth and paid a price for it.

What is something you knew you shouldn't do but did anyway?

HINDSIGHT

Tell a story about getting lost.

....

....

....

....

....

....

....

....

....

....

....

....

....

....

....

....

....

....

HINDSIGHT

What is an item you lost that you wish you had back?

HINDSIGHT

Who is someone you've fallen out of touch with and would like to reconnect with?

....

....

....

....

....

....

....

....

....

....

....

....

....

....

....

....

....

....

HINDSIGHT

If you could spend a day with a friend or
relative who has died, who would it be
and what would you do?

....

....

....

....

....

....

....

....

....

....

....

....

....

....

....

....

....

HINDSIGHT

Describe a special event that somehow
went wrong—for instance, a wedding
or graduation.

....
....
....
....
....
....
....
....
....
....
....
....
....
....
....
....

HINDSIGHT

What still shocks you?

HINDSIGHT

Is there a dramatic fight you had with your parents that could've been avoided?

....

....

....

....

....

....

....

....

....

....

....

....

....

....

....

....

....

....

What personal injustice still sticks with you? Is there an injustice you witnessed, or wished you'd intervened in?

HINDSIGHT

Do you have any regrets? What can you change now to address them?

....

....

....

....

....

....

....

....

....

....

....

....

....

....

....

....

....

....

THE BIG QUESTIONS

Describe an experience that changed your
mind about a strongly held opinion.

THE BIG QUESTIONS

What is happiness?

....

....

....

....

....

....

....

....

....

....

....

....

....

....

....

....

....

....

THE BIG QUESTIONS

When you were younger,
what were you told success was?
How has it changed over time?

THE BIG QUESTIONS

Was it important to you to have children?
Why or why not?

· ·

· ·

· ·

· ·

· ·

· ·

· ·

· ·

· ·

· ·

· ·

· ·

· ·

· ·

· ·

· ·

· ·

What did you want to change about the
way you raised your children, versus how
your parents raised you?

THE BIG QUESTIONS

How has raising children differed from what you expected?

· ·

· ·

· ·

· ·

· ·

· ·

· ·

· ·

· ·

· ·

· ·

· ·

· ·

· ·

· ·

· ·

· ·

How is your life different from the life
your parents had?

THE BIG QUESTIONS

What informed your sense
of right and wrong?

THE BIG QUESTIONS

What is the meaning of life?

THE BIG QUESTIONS

What's your favorite vice? Why?

THE BIG QUESTIONS

What would the title of your autobiography be?

THE BIG QUESTIONS

If you could know what the future held for
you, would you want to know it?
Why or why not?

. . . .

. . . .

. . . .

. . . .

. . . .

. . . .

. . . .

. . . .

. . . .

. . . .

. . . .

. . . .

. . . .

. . . .

. . . .

. . . .

. . . .

THE BIG QUESTIONS

What do you feel when you look up at the night sky?

THE BIG QUESTIONS

Do you think life on other planets is a
possibility? Have you ever seen a UFO or
something unusual in the sky?

THE BIG QUESTIONS

If you could ask an extraterrestrial one
question, what would it be?

THE BIG QUESTIONS

Have you ever seen a ghost or something unexplained?

THE BIG QUESTIONS

If you could ask someone who has
died one question, who would it be
and what would you ask?

THE BIG QUESTIONS

Do you believe in God? Why or why not?

....

....

....

....

....

....

....

....

....

....

....

....

....

....

....

....

....

....

How have your views on faith and
spirituality changed over time?

THE BIG QUESTIONS

Were you ever given proof of God, or had a religious experience?

THE BIG QUESTIONS

If you could ask God one question,
what would it be?

THE BIG QUESTIONS

What would heaven be to you?

....

....

....

....

....

....

....

....

....

....

....

....

....

....

....

....

....

THE BIG QUESTIONS

What would hell be?

THE BIG QUESTIONS

Do you believe in past lives? Who or what
do you think you were in a past life?

....

....

....

....

....

....

....

....

....

....

....

....

....

....

....

....

....

What might you want to
do in a future life?

THE BIG QUESTIONS

Would you want to live forever?
Why or why not?

If yes, in what way would you
want to live forever?

THE BIG QUESTIONS

What do you think happens after you die?

THE BIG QUESTIONS

How has the world changed in ways that you did not predict?

THE BIG QUESTIONS

How do you want to be remembered?

. . . .

. . . .

. . . .

. . . .

. . . .

. . . .

. . . .

. . . .

. . . .

. . . .

. . . .

. . . .

. . . .

. . . .

. . . .

. . . .

. . . .

. . . .

THE BIG QUESTIONS

What do you want your funeral to be like?

THE BIG QUESTIONS

What do you think is the ultimate future of humanity?

THE BIG QUESTIONS

What questions do you wish this book had asked?

THE BIG QUESTIONS

Notes:

....

....

....

....

....

....

....

....

....

....

....

....

....

....

....

....

....

....

Notes:

Thanks to everyone who supported us on Kickstarter, especially:

Jason Finn
Cyndy Perry Fletcher
Jennifer Loterbauer
Romona Perrault
Brian Reilly
Dan Schwenk
Diana Small
Laura Stratford
Scott and Holly Stratford
Gary Wright

Thank you all for your love and enthusiasm!

About the Authors

Robert K. Elder is the author, co-author or editor of more than 20 books. His work has appeared in the *New York Times*, *Los Angeles Times*, *Chicago Tribune*, *Boston Globe*, the *Paris Review*, and many other publications. Robert lives and writes in Chicagoland. Find out more at robertkelder.com.

Sasha Schwenk is a first-time author, although she has written many florid phrases in journals and letters, kept a travel blog during a grand European tour, and has been known to fire off a concise email. She's a former cheesemonger (a curd nerd, if you will), and current bird nerd, living in Portland, Oregon. She has binoculars on her at all times, in case of emergency birding.